DO IT YOURSELF BOOKS

MAKE YOUR OWN MUSICAL INSTRUMENTS

Margaret McLean

illustrated by Ken Stott

Lerner Publications Company • Minneapolis

This edition of this book is available in two bindings:
Library binding by Lerner Publications Company
Soft cover by First Avenue Editions
241 First Avenue North
Minneapolis, Minnesota 55401

This edition first published 1988 by Lerner Publications Company

Library of Congress Cataloging-in-Publication Data

McLean, Margaret.
    Make your own musical instruments.

    (Do it yourself books)
    Previously published as: Making musical instruments.
    Summary: Step-by-step directions for making a
variety of musical instruments, such as tambourine,
drum, xylophone, recorder; and a simple explanation
of basic music notation and rhythm.
    1. Musical instruments—Construction—Juvenile
literature. [1. Musical instruments—Construction]
I. Stott, Ken, ill. II. Title. III. Series.
ML460.M4   1988   781.91   87-29670
    ISBN 0-8225-0895-8 (lib. bdg.)
    ISBN 0-8225-9558-3 (pbk.)

Manufactured in the United States of America

2   3   4   5   6   7   8   9   10   97   96   95   94   93   92   91   90   89

MAKE YOUR OWN MUSICAL INSTRUMENTS

Making music is something we should all be able to enjoy without having to be trained musicians. Music is even more rewarding when you can pick out favorite tunes on an instrument you designed and built yourself. There is something here for everyone, whether it's the construction side that interests you most or you simply enjoy exploring sound. Start with something simple like a maraca, then as you become more confident using tools, move on to the more ambitious projects. Devote as much time and care as you can to making your instruments as the results will be worth it.

CONTENTS

INSTRUMENTS AND SOUND

There are three main groups or classes of musical instruments – wind, string and percussion. All three types have existed for thousands of years. We know this from ancient wall paintings that show people playing instruments not at all unlike our modern ones. A few instruments are difficult to classify. The piano, for example, is both a stringed and a percussive instrument since its sound is produced by felt-covered hammers striking strings.

This book shows you how to make homemade versions of real instruments. You may not be able to match them for quality of sound or range of notes, but you should be able to pick out rhythms of a good tune.

STRINGS

The basic principle behind all stringed instruments is the same – thin strands of wire or gut are made to vibrate over a sound box.

Bow

Violin

Classical guitar

Orchestral instruments, like the violin, are normally played with bows. Solo instruments, like the classical guitar, are plucked with the fingers or a plectrum.

PERCUSSION

The percussion section of an orchestra is made up of tuned and untuned instruments that sound when struck. The kettledrums are tuned to a definite pitch by turning handles on the rim. Other instruments include tubular bells, xylophones, gongs and triangles.

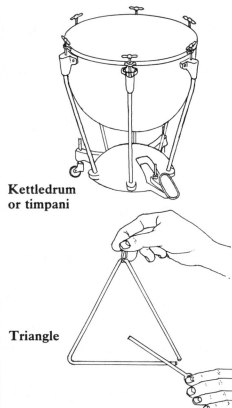

Kettledrum or timpani

Triangle

Percussion

There is almost no limit to the different kinds of percussion instruments you can make. It will depend on the materials you have available.

WIND

When you blow into any wind instrument, the sound is produced because you are making columns of air vibrate. In the oboe, this is caused by reeds. Reeds are simply strips of metal or cane that can vibrate. The flute has no reed, but a jet of air blown across the mouth hole sets up the vibration. With a trumpet, the shape of the mouthpiece makes the lips vibrate as the player blows. This makes the air in the instrument vibrate.

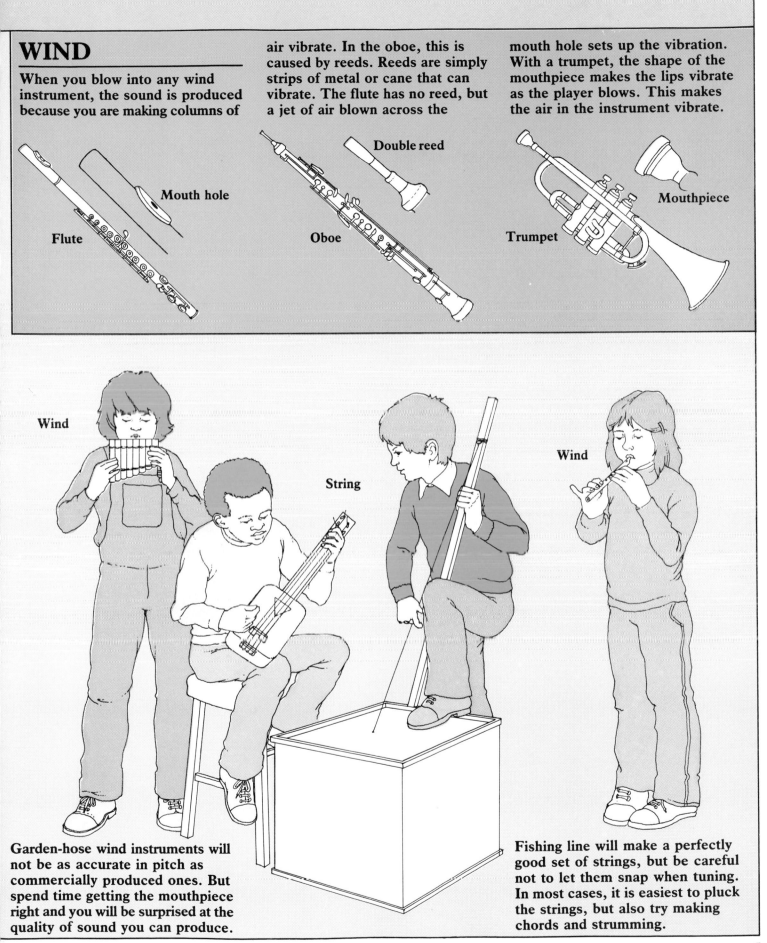

Mouth hole

Flute

Double reed

Oboe

Mouthpiece

Trumpet

Wind

String

Wind

Garden-hose wind instruments will not be as accurate in pitch as commercially produced ones. But spend time getting the mouthpiece right and you will be surprised at the quality of sound you can produce.

Fishing line will make a perfectly good set of strings, but be careful not to let them snap when tuning. In most cases, it is easiest to pluck the strings, but also try making chords and strumming.

MATERIALS AND TOOLS

Musical instruments can be made from all sorts of odds and ends lying around the house or garden. With a few basic skills and a bit of imagination, you should be able to make up a miniature orchestra, or at least a band. It's worth remembering, though, that making instruments is a craft, and one that will improve with practice. So don't rush things, pay attention to detail, and the results will be worth it.

Take great care when using tools. If you're not sure how to handle them – ask. Build up a collection of nails, screws and tacks and keep them in a box along with your tools.

Wooden instruments will look even more attractive if you varnish them. You can decorate anything made of tin with stickers, or use enamel paint.

TOOLS

Here are a few of the tools you may have to use when making your instruments. The saws in particular may be difficult to handle, so ask an adult to help you. The large hand saw is used for cutting wood to length, while a coping saw is best for cutting out shapes. For cutting plastic or cardboard, use a Stanley knife.

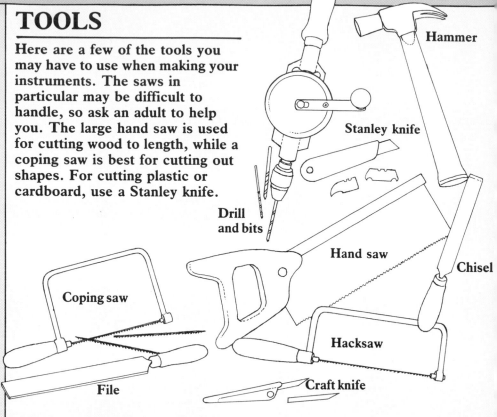

Hammer

Stanley knife

Drill and bits

Hand saw

Chisel

Coping saw

Hacksaw

File

Craft knife

A WORK BENCH

A sturdy kitchen table makes an ideal work bench, although any fairly large table will do. Protect the table top with a sheet of hardboard. Keep tools and materials within easy reach and tidy up as you go along.

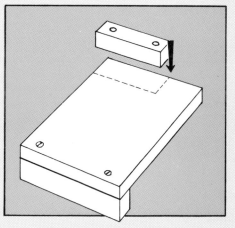

Wood is best held in place by a vise or clamp. If you do not have one, try making a simple bench hook as shown. To use it, place the bottom block against the work bench and hold the wood to be sawn firmly against the top of block.

ADVICE ON TOOLS

Whatever tool you are using, be very careful. Keep fingers well clear of sharp blades and don't swing wildly with a hammer. Never leave tools lying around.

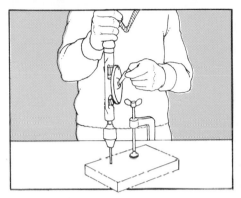

The "bits" of a drill make holes of different sizes. Steady the drill while turning the handle.

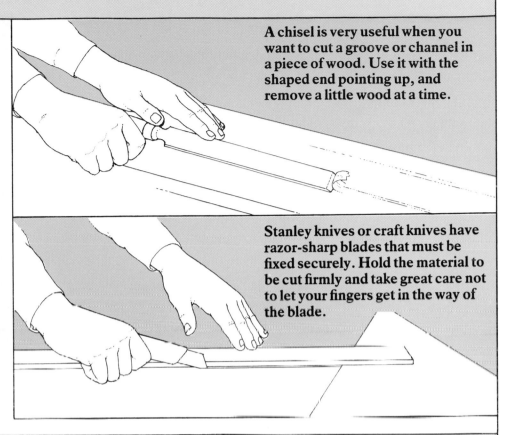

A chisel is very useful when you want to cut a groove or channel in a piece of wood. Use it with the shaped end pointing up, and remove a little wood at a time.

Stanley knives or craft knives have razor-sharp blades that must be fixed securely. Hold the material to be cut firmly and take great care not to let your fingers get in the way of the blade.

THINGS TO COLLECT

Before you go out and buy any of the materials suggested in the book, see what is available at home. Be inventive. If you cannot obtain the particular materials suggested, try something similar that *is* available. You may find it works just as well! *From the kitchen:* plastic bottles; cookie tins; yogurt containers; earthenware casseroles; wooden spoons; straws; popsicle sticks; screw-cap bottles; corks. *Garden equipment:* earthenware flowerpots; garden hose. *Building materials:* pieces of wood; dowels; paintbrushes; metal tubing; bamboo cane. *Odds and ends:* modeling dope; fishing line; adhesive bonding glue; nails; screws and tacks; packing tape; scissors; foam insulator tape; strong brown paper; string; eyelet screws; beads; paperclips.

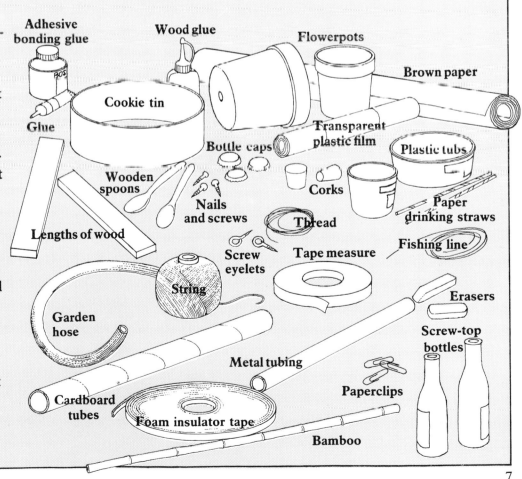

SIMPLE PERCUSSION

The percussion section of any modern symphony orchestra contains a large variety of instruments. Some are tuned and some are untuned, but all of them produce their sound when struck, either with the hand or with some kind of stick. The simplest instrument of all is a set of claves, or rhythm sticks. They consist of two small, solid cylinders of wood which are banged together. Sand blocks are simply blocks of wood wrapped in sandpaper that produce a soft shuffling noise when rubbed against one another.

Interesting sounds can be produced with the most everyday objects. Try rolling peas up and down a tray – it can sound just like rain. Add thunder by shaking a sheet of metal. Many sound effects used in radio plays and stories are produced in a similar way.

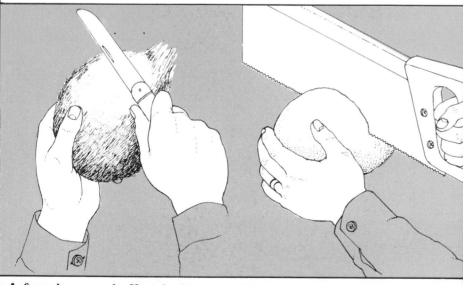

Fold the sandpaper into neat pleats at the corner

SAND BLOCKS

You will need: 2 blocks of wood approximately 5 × 4 × 1 inches (12 × 10 × 2 cm); 2 small pieces of wood; sandpaper; tacks; glue.
For handles, glue the small pieces of wood to the center of the larger blocks. Wrap sandpaper around the wood and secure with tacks.

COCONUT SHELLS

A favorite sound effect is the clatter of horses' hooves on hard ground. The sound is best reproduced with coconut shells. The outside shell, or husk, of a coconut is covered in prickly bristles. Scrape these off carefully with a sharp knife until you are left with the inner hard part of the shell. If you haven't already done so, remember to make a hole and let the milk out!

The next step is to cut the coconut in two. This is not easy, as coconuts are very hard to saw through. Besides this, a coconut is too big to go in a vise. So, ask an adult to cut the coconut for you. You can help by steadying the coconut as it is being sawn.

When you have your two halves, scrape out all the coconut pulp. Leave the shells to dry out thoroughly.

Clasp the shells in each of your hands. Gently click the edges of the shells together until it sounds like a horse walking or trotting.

CLAVES

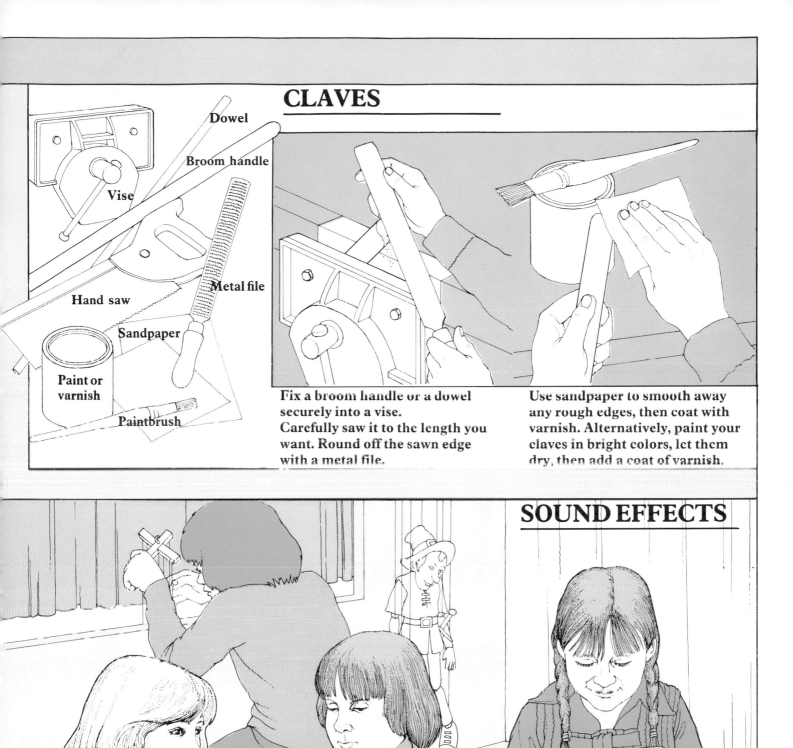

Fix a broom handle or a dowel securely into a vise.
Carefully saw it to the length you want. Round off the sawn edge with a metal file.

Use sandpaper to smooth away any rough edges, then coat with varnish. Alternatively, paint your claves in bright colors, let them dry, then add a coat of varnish.

SOUND EFFECTS

Making up your own sound effects can be a lot of fun. Try acting out a story with dolls or puppets and see how many different sounds you can create.

MARACAS AND CASTANETS

Rattles, in one form or another, are found in many societies throughout the world. They often play an important role in religious ceremonies, including witch doctor magic.

Maracas are a well-known form of rattle used to great effect in Latin-American rumba bands. They are gourds filled with dried seeds which rustle as the instrument is shaken.

Castanets belong to the same family of instruments as the cymbals. Both consist of two hollowed-out surfaces which are clashed against one another to produce the sound. However, castanets are usually made of wood while cymbals are always made of metal. Spanish flamenco dancers play castanets with great skill against the palm of the hand.

CASTANETS

You will need: 4 identical wooden spoons; narrow elastic tape; hacksaw; drill; sandpaper for smoothing.

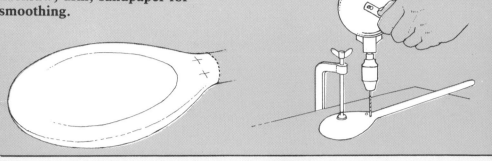

On each spoon, draw a line 1 inch (2.5 cm) up the handle. Just below, mark the position of two holes through which you will thread the elastic.

With the spoons firmly clamped, drill through the holes you have marked. Try to make all the holes the same size and evenly spread.

MARACAS

The maracas make a very distinctive hissing noise that sounds like a wave gently washing over a pebble beach. It is a sound you can easily pick out in Latin-American rumba or samba music.

For homemade maracas, you will need: Yogurt containers, strainers, or liquid detergent bottles; masking tape; dowels; strong brown paper; filling materials.

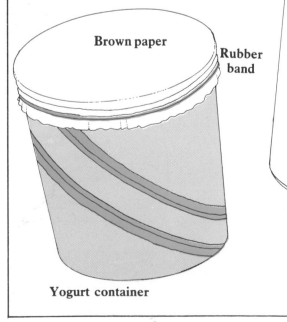

Brown paper

Rubber band

Yogurt container

Liquid detergent bottle

Dowel

Tape

Two strainers, with the bowls facing each other

Tape

Whatever container you decide to use for your maraca, make sure it is completely dry before adding your filling. Try handfuls of dried peas, beans, lentils, rice or gravel. Now seal your container firmly – you don't want the contents to spill out with the first shake! Finally, add your own decoration.

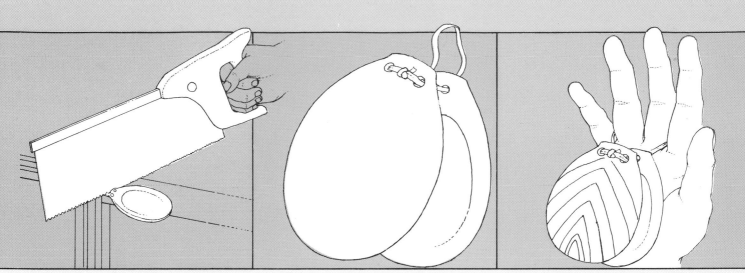

Clamp each spoon in turn and saw along the line you have drawn. (A hacksaw is best.) Smooth the sawn ends.

Put two spoons together with the bowls facing each other. Thread the elastic through, leaving a loop on one side. Tie the ends.

Slip the loop over your middle finger so that the spoons rest inside your palm. Try to make a "click," not simply a rattle.

BLOCK CASTANETS

Few orchestral percussion players have mastered the art of playing castanets in the palm of the hand. They are far more likely to use block castanets, which are quicker and easier to learn to play. In this version of the instrument, the two sides of the castanet clack against a central block of wood.

You will need: 3 pieces of wood, one about 6 inches (15 cm) long and fairly thin, and two smaller pieces; string; coping saw and drill.

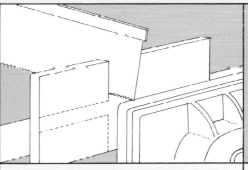

Pencil in the handle shape on the largest piece of wood as shown. With the wood firmly clamped, use the coping saw to cut around the shapes. Sand down rough edges.

Drill two holes in each of the blocks of wood as shown. You must make sure that all the sets of holes line up perfectly, so take care with your measurements.

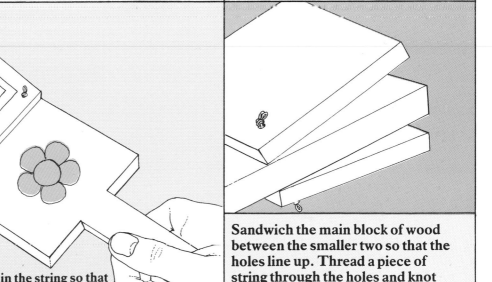

Leave enough slack in the string so that the bits of wood can flap freely

Sandwich the main block of wood between the smaller two so that the holes line up. Thread a piece of string through the holes and knot the ends.

TAMBOURINE AND JINGLING JOHNNIE

Jingles are small bells which are found in different forms all over the world. They can be made of bones, nuts or bits of metal – basically, anything that will make a jingling sound when joined together. Traditional dancers sometimes attach jingles to various parts of their body. A temple dancer from the Indonesian island of Bali, for example, wears ankle bells while an English Morris dancer wears bells around the knees.

Both the instruments shown here make use of jingles. The Jingling Johnnie was originally a Turkish military-band instrument, but today you will probably only see one at folk festivals. The tambourine is Middle-Eastern but was brought to Europe about 700 years ago. It is a type of small drum with metal jingling discs around the rim. It is particularly popular with folk-singers and folk-dancing troupes.

JINGLING JOHNNIE

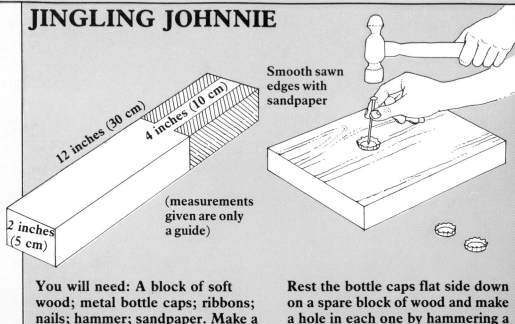

(measurements given are only a guide)

Smooth sawn edges with sandpaper

You will need: A block of soft wood; metal bottle caps; ribbons; nails; hammer; sandpaper. Make a handle shape by cutting out the shaded area with a fretsaw.

Rest the bottle caps flat side down on a spare block of wood and make a hole in each one by hammering a sharp nail through it.

TAMBOURINE

1: Begin by carefully removing the bottom of an old cake or cookie tin with a can opener. Watch out for your fingers on the jagged edge!

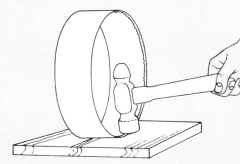

2: Rest the shell of the tin on its side on a block of wood or work surface. Now hammer down the sharp edge to make it neater.

There are various ways to play the tambourine. Different volumes of tone can be obtained by tapping the skin with the fingertips, knuckles, or palm of the hand. It is also possible to make the tambourine vibrate by wetting your thumb and running it around the edge of the skin.

You will need: A cookie tin; metal bottle caps; paper fasteners or paperclips; strong brown paper; masking tape; scissors; hammer; nail.

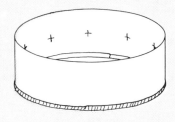

3: Put masking or insulating tape over the hammered edge. Mark with crosses where the jingles are going to go.

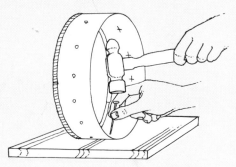

4: Rest the tin on its side and make the holes for the jingles by hammering a sharp nail through on to a wooden board.

5: Prepare the bottle caps like you did for the Jingling Johnnie. Push through a paper fastener or unbent paperclip.

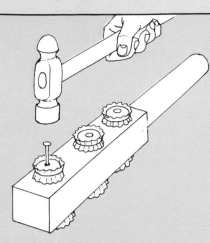

When you have as many jingles as you want, paint them with a bright enamel paint. Nail some ribbons to the top as a finishing touch, and you are ready to play.

Don't just stand there shaking the instrument – it's fun to dance at the same time. Try dancing around the maypole on May Day.

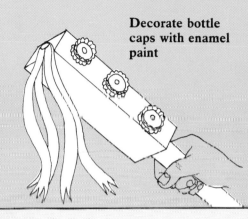

Decorate bottle caps with enamel paint

Put two bottle caps back to back and push a short nail through both. Hammer them gently into the sides of the shaped wooden block. Do not push them right in, as they must be able to "jingle."

TAMBOURINE

Paint a design over the tape or use stickers

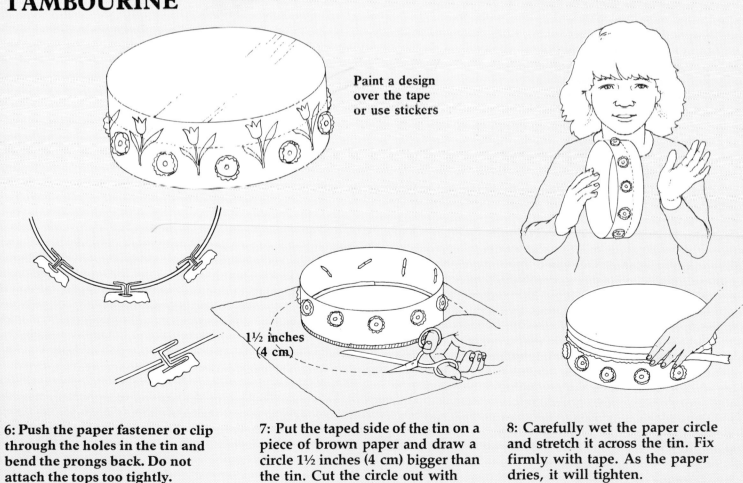

1½ inches (4 cm)

6: Push the paper fastener or clip through the holes in the tin and bend the prongs back. Do not attach the tops too tightly.

7: Put the taped side of the tin on a piece of brown paper and draw a circle 1½ inches (4 cm) bigger than the tin. Cut the circle out with scissors.

8: Carefully wet the paper circle and stretch it across the tin. Fix firmly with tape. As the paper dries, it will tighten.

INSTRUMENTS FROM POTS AND TUBS

Earthenware pots and plastic tubs can be turned into a whole host of un-usual instruments. They may not be the sort of instruments you would find in an orchestra, but they will produce a variety of distinctive sounds. The friction drum is found in different forms in many parts of the world. The sound is made not by striking the drum with a beater, but by rubbing a stick fixed upright into the drum skin.

The washtub bass was one of the earliest pop group instruments. Even the one-string version (shown here) provides a good rhythm. It is a simple version of the orchestral double bass. The latter is the largest and lowest-note stringed instrument in an orch-estra. It usually has four strings.

FRICTION DRUMS

You will need: A clean, dry plastic pot (a yogurt container is ideal); string; a hole-puncher or scissors; bright enamel paint or stickers.

Drill hole and thread string through

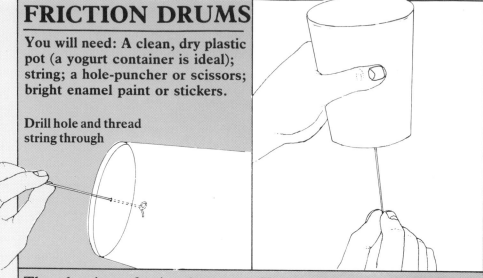

Thread a piece of string through a hole in the bottom of the pot.

Hold the pot and pull the string up and down to make it "talk."

WASHTUB BASS

A washtub bass can employ any large hollow container for its sound box, not just a washtub. To play the instrument, hook the notched stick over the rim of the tub. Brace it with one foot and pull the stick backwards and forwards to alter the tension of the string. Pluck with your other hand.

You will need: A large container as a resonator (metal washtub, crate, garbage can or wastepaper basket); some thick cord; a notched stick (an old clothes-line prop is ideal); drill.

Wind free end of string around several times and knot tightly

Washtub

String attached to peg or dowel

Garbage can

ROMMELPOT

The rommelpot is another kind of friction drum. It is featured in the Christmas or New Year celebrations of several European countries. Traditionally, children play the pot and ask for gifts for it, not themselves!

You will need: A round, earthenware casserole dish; heavy plastic film or clear contact paper; a dowel, about 12 inches (30 cm) long; lots of string; scissors.

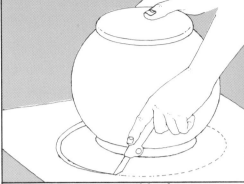

1: Place the pot upside-down on the paper side of the heavy plastic film. Draw around the rim of the pot, then draw another circle 4 inches (10 cm) larger. Cut out the large circle.

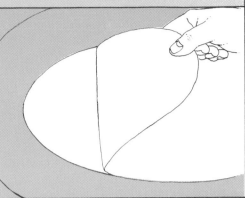

2: Carefully cut around the paper covering of the inner circle and peel back. Leave the sticky surface of the outer circle covered for the time being.

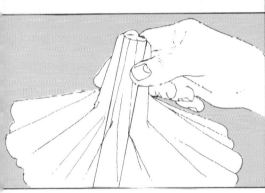

3: Push the dowel gently into the center of the non-sticky side of the circle. DON'T poke it right through. Stretch the film taut over the tip of the stick.

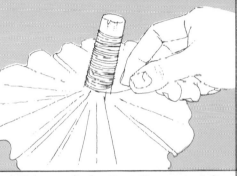

4: To attach the dowel, you need to bind, or whip, the plastic over the dowel with string. Secure firmly so that the dowel cannot work loose from the dish.

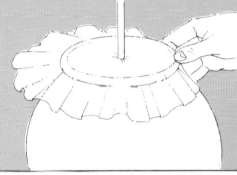

5: Now remove the rest of the backing. Center the plastic – sticky side down! – over the open end of the pot. The dowel should stand more or less straight up.

6: Go around pulling the plastic so that it's absolutely taut. There should be no wrinkles anywhere. Now wet a piece of string and wind it several times round the rim. As the string dries, it will shrink and so the "skin" will become even tighter.

To play your rommelpot, tuck it under one arm. Wet your free hand and gently slide it up and down the dowel. See how many different noises you can produce.

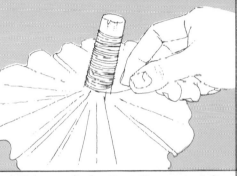

SIMPLE DRUMS

Drums come in all shapes and sizes, from the huge orchestral bass drum to the hand-held tabor. They can be round, cylindrical, bowl-shaped or waisted, and they can have a single or a double skin. Usually, only one of the skins, or membranes, is struck; the second one acts as a resonator. The traditional material for a drum skin is calf vellum, but modern drums often use plastic.

Simple kinds of drums produce only one note. That note will vary, however, if the tension of the skin changes. In humid conditions the vellum will slacken and the pitch of the note will drop. One advantage of plastic drum heads is that they are not affected by changing weather.

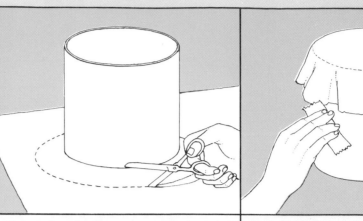

For a simple drum you will need: A large coffee can; strong brown paper; masking tape; scissors. Cut a paper circle 4 inches (10 cm) larger than the diameter of the can.

Dampen the paper circle with water, and then center it over the open end of the can. Fix lightly in place with a couple of pieces of masking tape.

PRAYER DRUM

Prayer drums are common throughout the Far East. They form part of the ritual of religious ceremonies. The Indonesian version shown here has a double-sided head stretched over a light, shallow frame.

You will need: A round, wooden cheese box (the sort Camembert comes in, *not* the floppy cream cheese sort); strong brown paper; masking tape; fine cord or string; small rubber or wooden beads; a piece of dowel; Stanley knife.

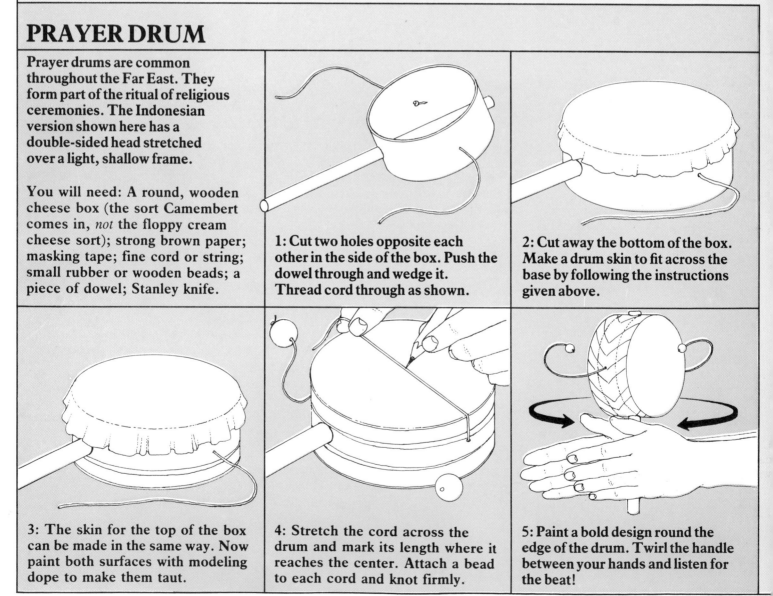

1: Cut two holes opposite each other in the side of the box. Push the dowel through and wedge it. Thread cord through as shown.

2: Cut away the bottom of the box. Make a drum skin to fit across the base by following the instructions given above.

3: The skin for the top of the box can be made in the same way. Now paint both surfaces with modeling dope to make them taut.

4: Stretch the cord across the drum and mark its length where it reaches the center. Attach a bead to each cord and knot firmly.

5: Paint a bold design round the edge of the drum. Twirl the handle between your hands and listen for the beat!

Make pleats, or folds, in the paper to ease out the fullness. When the surface of your drum skin is taut, wrap strong tape firmly around the edges.

Your drum will produce a clearer note if you paint the paper surface with modeling dope first. When it is dry, add decorations to your own design.

Modeling dope

TUNED DRUM KIT

Drums made out of different-sized containers produce notes of different pitch. They sound best when raised off the ground, so arrange them around a circular coffee table or similar support. First, cut out a circle of corrugated cardboard that overhangs the table by about 4 inches (10 cm) all around. Cut flaps into this 4-inch (10-cm) fringe as shown.

Tape the drums, in order of pitch, to the flaps and rest the cardboard over the table.

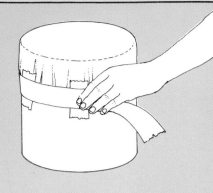

Corrugated cardboard with flaps

4 inches (10 cm)

Flap

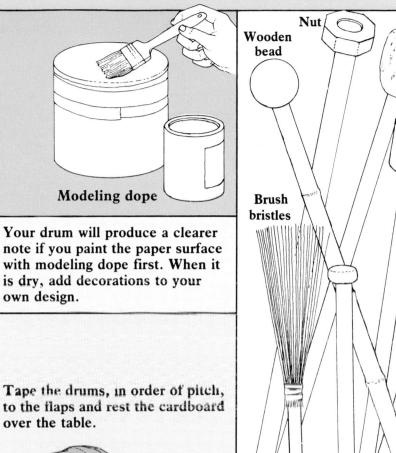

Wooden bead

Nut

Cork

Tape

Brush bristles

String

Shaped dowel

Bamboo

Knitting needle

BEATERS

Each of the homemade drumsticks shown here will produce a very different quality of sound from the same drum. Wind felt strips around the top of a knitting needle for a soft sound; for a harder sound try rubber or wooden beads. Drum brushes produce a rustling noise.

TENSIONED DRUMS

The marching tempo of a military band is usually provided by side drums. These are small drums with a skin at either end of a shallow cylinder. The drummer holds the instrument slightly to one side of the body and beats out the rhythm with drumsticks on the upper skin. At the same time, lengths of gut or wire stretched across the lower skin vibrate. This produces the distinctive rattling sound of the drum. The wires (known as snares) can be released if a more muted tone is required.

Quite a different sound is produced by the double-skin waisted drum. Some West African people produce a whole octave of notes by pressing the lacing that joins the two skins.

For a skin you will need: Muslin; fine cord; adhesive bonding glue; hammer; nail; ruler; pencil; scissors.

DRUM SKIN

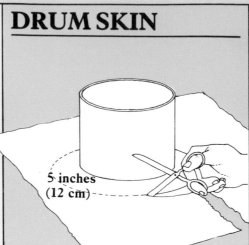

1: Place your drum can on top of the muslin and draw around the can. Go around the circle marking points 5 inches (12 cm) out from the edge to make a larger circle. Cut this out and use it to cut another circle.

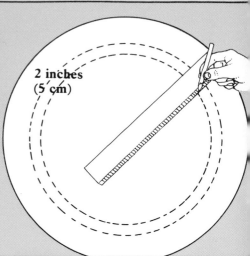

2: Mark the center of each circle and place a ruler from the center to the edge as shown. Pencil two dots, one 1 inch (2.5 cm) in from the edge, the other 2 inches (5 cm) in. Go around until each "skin" has two inner circles.

SIDE DRUM

The side drum shown here has no snares as it is difficult to get them to work properly in a homemade instrument. Muslin or an old sheet can be used for the skins.

You will need: A large coffee can; 2 drum skins; long length of cord; shoelaces.

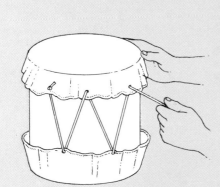

1: Remove the bottom of the can with a can opener. Dampen both skins and the lashing cord. Tie a knot in one end of the cord and thread the two skins together.

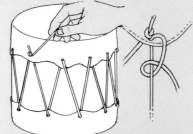

2: Go all the way around until all the holes have been laced and the skins are stretched tightly across both ends. Make a firm knot at the first hole as shown.

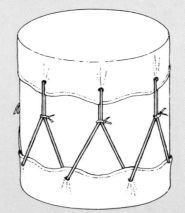

3: To keep the drum skins at the right tension, loop small pieces of leather or shoelaces around two laces at a time as shown. Move the loops up and down to stretch the skins tight for a better sound.

Cord sling attached to drum lace

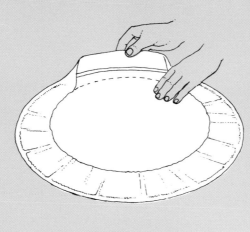

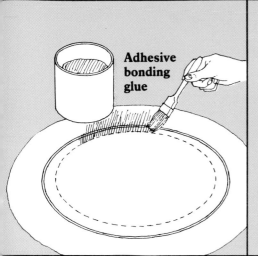

3: Cut a piece of cord to fit on the first inner circle. Join the ends with tape to make a ring. Brush adhesive bonding glue from the edge to the second line. Repeat.

4: Fold the outer edge of the muslin over the cord and press firmly until well stuck. Repeat with the second skin. Place under a heavy book or other weight and allow ten minutes to dry.

5: On each skin, mark eight dots the same distance apart just inside the cord rim on the glued part. With a nail or bradawl, punch holes through the dots large enough to take the lashing cord.

WAISTED DRUM

In the past, waisted drums were important as tom-toms, or talking drums. Today, there is a wide variety of designs and playing techniques. West African and Japanese waisted drums are particularly elaborate.

You will need: 2 earthenware flowerpots; cord; 2 popsicle sticks; pieces of wire; 2 skins.

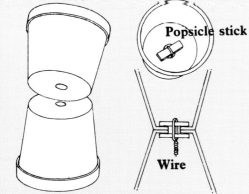

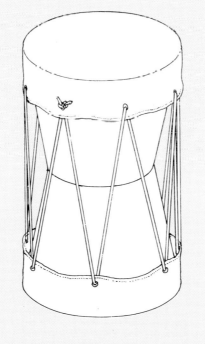

Join the two flowerpots at their bases by twisting a piece of wire around a popsicle stick placed at the bottom of each pot. Twist until the pots are secured tightly and there is little wobble.

Before attaching the skins, wrap some masking tape around the rim of both flowerpots to prevent rubbing. Lash in the same way as the side drum. Play by tensioning the laces between the knees.

BOTTLE XYLOPHONE AND FLOWERPOT CHIMES

Glass containers, such as drinking glasses, jars and bottles, produce different notes when tapped lightly on the side. Depending on the size of the vessel and its quality, you will get a bright or dull sound. Delicate china cups, for example, will sound quite different from milk bottles. The pitch of the notes can be altered by adding water to the containers. If you experiment with various containers of different sizes, you should get a large enough range of notes to play simple tunes.

The bottle xylophone is just a sophisticated version of the water chimes described above. To make the instrument easier to play, the bottles are sealed and laid across a frame so that they can be struck from above like a true xylophone.

XYLOPHONE

For your bottle xylophone you will need: 8 screwtop or corked bottles of the same size (corks may need to be sealed with candlewax); 4 strips of wood; foam insulator tape; glue; nails; hammer; hand saw; water.

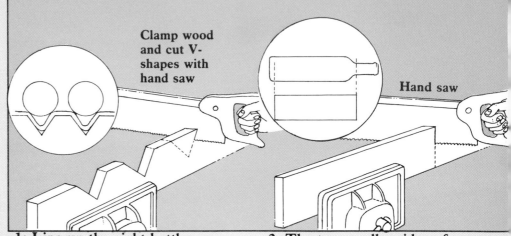

Clamp wood and cut V-shapes with hand saw

Hand saw

1: Line up the eight bottles on their sides. Cut two strips of wood twice as long as the row of bottles. Pencil in eight V-shaped notches wide enough to hold the bottles.

2: The two smaller sides of your frame do not need notches. Simply measure two strips of wood against one of the bottles as shown. Saw off the lengths required.

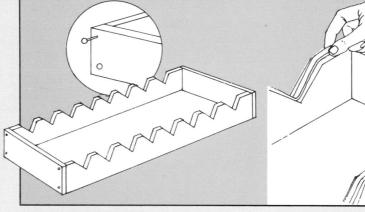

3: Glue the edges of the frame and press them together firmly as shown. When the glue has dried, carefully pound in two nails at each corner to make the frame extra strong.

4: To stop the bottles rolling around, fix small strips of foam insulator tape along the top of the frame. This also improves the quality of the notes.

5: Stick pieces of rubber or felt to the bottom corners of the frame. Now lay the bottles across the notched sides of the completed frame. There should be a gap between each bottle to obtain the purest note in each case.

TUNING

Different notes can be produced from the bottles by adding different amounts of water. It is quite difficult to be precise about tuning. The easiest thing to do is to fill one bottle with water nearly to the brim, and call it "do." To get "re," fill up a second bottle with water and pour out small amounts until the note sounds right. Repeat the process with each bottle in turn until an eight-note scale is produced. It is a good idea to put a sticky label on each bottle marked with the name of its note.

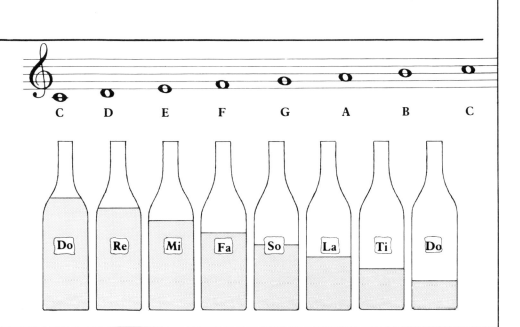

FLOWERPOT CHIMES

If you know anyone who has a lot of earthenware flowerpots, try to persuade them to let you examine them for their quality of pitch. Flowerpots do have a very bell-like sound. Give each pot a gentle tap and see if you can make up a scale. Hang them from an old broom handle as in the picture, then see if you can play a duet with the bottle xylophonist!

Dowel acts
as brace

WOODEN XYLOPHONE AND TUBULAR BELLS

A xylophone is basically a set of wooden bars of different lengths which are played with beaters. The sound obtained depends on various factors – what type of wood is used, how thick the wood is, and what kind of beater is employed.

Tubular bells are made not of wood, but metal tubing. Like the xylophone, lengths are graded to give different notes. In Tchaikovsky's *1812 Overture*, they are played to sound like the thunderous peal of church bells.

For the xylophone you will need: Strips of hardwood, such as oak – some 1 inch (2.5 cm) wide ×¼ inch (0.5 cm) deep and some 1¼ inch (3 cm) wide ×½ inch (1.5 cm) deep; foam insulator tape: short nails; glue; hammer; drill; hacksaw.

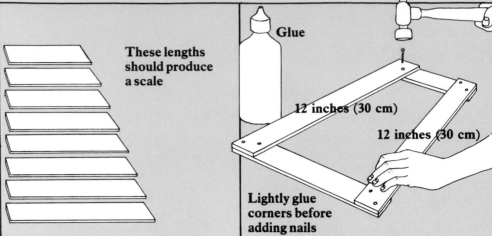

These lengths should produce a scale

Glue

12 inches (30 cm)

12 inches (30 cm)

Lightly glue corners before adding nails

Using the 1-inch (2.5-cm)-wide wood, cut a strip 10 inches (25 cm) long. Tune it to 'C' on the piano (see Tuning). Cut seven more bars, each about ¾ inch (2 cm) shorter than the one before.

Using the 1¼-inch (3-cm)-wide wood, saw off four lengths: two about 12 inches (30 cm) long, one half as long as your longest bar, and one half as long as your shortest bar.

TUBULAR BELLS

Saw off a piece of tube 11 inches (28 cm) long. This should give you 'C', more or less. If the note's too high, you will have to cut a longer tube; if it's too low, trim a bit off. Cut seven more tubes, each roughly 1 inch (2.5 cm) shorter than the one before it, to give you your octave.

You will need: copper tube, with ¾-inch (2-cm) bore; hacksaw; drill; string; a pole.

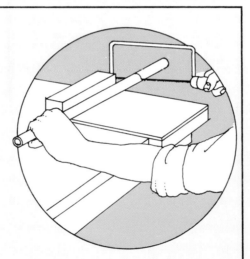

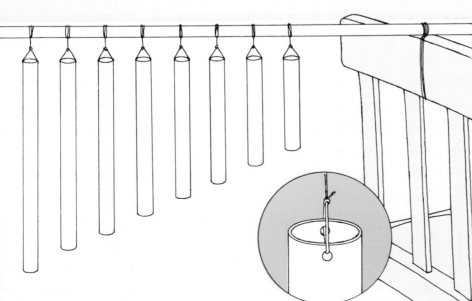

TUNING

Tuning your bars to a scale takes time and patience. You may cut off a length of wood that sounds nearly right, but not quite. If the note is too low, simply saw a small piece off the end of the bar. If it's too high, you can lower the note slightly by making a saw-cut in the bar.

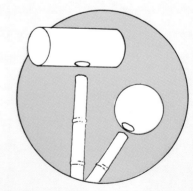

BEATERS

The best xylophone beaters consist of a wooden bead or piece of dowel glued onto a bamboo cane. You will need a fairly long length of bamboo to give a feeling of "bounce" as you strike the bars.

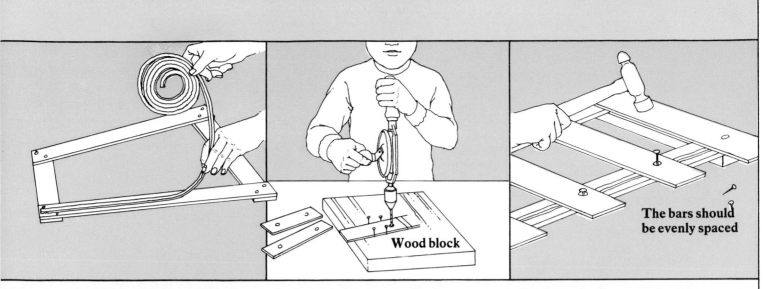

Place a strip of foam insulator tape on each of the longer sides of the frame. Your xylophone will give a better tone as a result.

Lay the bars across the frame, starting with the longest bar at the wide end. Mark where nails will attach each bar to the frame (see Tuning) and drill through.

Replace the bars on the frame and hammer a nail lightly through each hole. Don't pound the nails right in – the bars must vibrate slightly. Sand and varnish.

FINE ADJUSTMENTS

Test the sound each bar produces by laying them in order of length on a piece of rope or cord. Wooden bars have a "dead" spot about a quarter of the way in from each end.

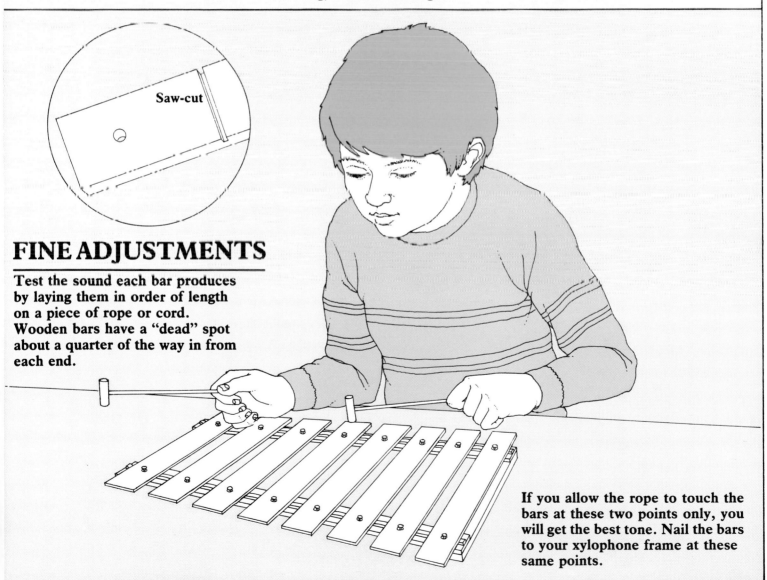

If you allow the rope to touch the bars at these two points only, you will get the best tone. Nail the bars to your xylophone frame at these same points.

SIMPLE WIND INSTRUMENTS

There are basically two ways in which sound is produced in wind instruments – either air is blown across a hole, as in the flute, or reeds are used. Blowing across a hole is not as easy as it sounds. Wind instrument players have to practice hard to get the "embouchure" right. (This is the word musicians use to describe the correct way of using the mouth and lips.) Try blowing across a cola bottle and see how difficult it is to get a good sound every time!

A reed is simply a thin, flexible blade which produces a sound when it vibrates. If you put two grass stems between your hands and blow hard, you should get a reed-like noise. When you are playing a double-reed instrument, try to force air between the reeds, or try using your tongue with a "tutting" sound. You might have to practice to perfect the sound.

FUN WITH REEDS

The easiest and certainly the cheapest way of trying out some reed effects is with some paper drinking straws. Flatten a section about ½ inch (1.5 cm) long at one end and snip into a point (a). Now blow hard between the two bits – you should get a "buzz." Once you have obtained a good, steady note, cut off bits from the opposite end of the straw while you blow. What happens?

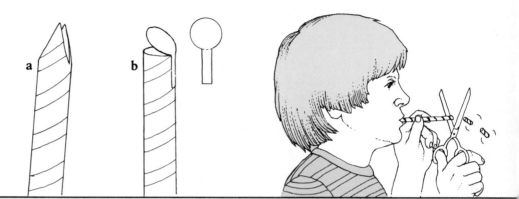

PANPIPES

Panpipes are basically a set of pipes joined together and blown across the top. They take their name from the god Pan, who was half man and half beast. His pipes were supposed to have the power to charm anything in the animal kingdom. Traditionally, Panpipes are made of bamboo, although you may find it a difficult material to work with. It is very hard to cut and the knots inside have to be burned out.

You will need: Garden hose; string or masking tape; craft knife.

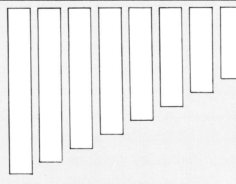

1: Cut off eight lengths of hose. Make each new length of hose about ¼ inch (0.5 cm) shorter than the one before it.

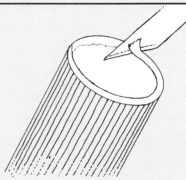

2: Cutting the playing edge is the most important part of the whole process. Use a craft knife to cut as sharp an edge as you can.

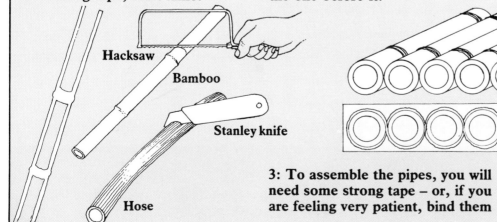

3: To assemble the pipes, you will need some strong tape – or, if you are feeling very patient, bind them with twine. The technique is a bit like lashing a raft together. Make as neat a job as you can.

When you have mastered the flattened straw technique, try adding a circular "reed" (b) to a longish tube, such as a piece of garden hose. Attach the circle so that it forms a lid on one end of the tube. Now blow!

KAZOO

You will need: a cardboard tube, plastic or waxed paper; masking tape.
First make four fingerholes. Wedge a piece of wood in the tube while you do this. Tape the paper over one end and blow down the other.

Cut holes against wood block

PLAYING TECHNIQUE

Blow across the top of your pipes, aiming a jet of air at the opposite side to where your lips are. Panpipes are not usually played as single notes; it's more common to blow right along the top so that a series of notes comes out.

Cork plug   Clay plug

TUNING

To tune the Panpipes, first plug a piece of cork or modeling clay in the bottom of each pipe so that no air can get through. Blow down each one to test its pitch. If a note is too high in the scale, push the plug down; if the note is too low, push the plug up into the pipe.

RECORDER AND SWANEE WHISTLE

The recorder is a type of woodwind instrument without a reed. It was well-known throughout the 16th to 18th centuries, before the flute gained in popularity. Today, there is a revival of interest in the recorder, and it is the first musical instrument many school children learn to play.

Recorders were originally made of wood but plastic ones are more common in schools. The most familiar is the soprano. Its lowest note is one octave above middle C. Next down in pitch is the alto, then the tenor, and finally the bass, which looks rather like a bassoon. It has a curved metal mouthpiece projecting from the top. The sopranino is pitched even higher than the soprano, but it is rarely played.

THE MOUTHPIECE

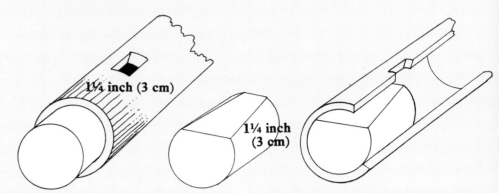

1¼ inch (3 cm)

1¼ inch (3 cm)

Carefully cut out an air-hole with a craft knife 1¼ inch (3 cm) in from one end of a piece of garden hose. Make sure the far side of the hole slopes away from you as shown.

Sand down a 1¼-inch-(3-cm)-long piece of dowel to give a smooth, slanting surface on one side. Insert into the hose, slanting side upwards, and try to blow a clear note.

RECORDER

You will need: Garden hose about 12 inches (30 cm) long, with a mouthpiece inserted in one end (as described above); a craft knife.

1: Cut off the hose to the length required to give middle C. Now measure the distance from the middle of your air hole to the bottom of the hose, say 12 inches (30 cm), and divide this figure by four (12 ÷ 4 = 3). In this case, your lowest fingerhole is then 3 inches (7.5 cm) in from the bottom of the hose, and your top fingerhole 3 inches (7.5 cm) down the hose, measured from the middle of your air hole.

2: Mark six equally spaced fingerholes (follow instruction 1 for how to calculate the position of the top and bottommost holes). Cut the holes, starting at the bottom. Make each hole bigger until it gives the next note of the scale.

3: Make the final hole for your thumb directly opposite your top hole. If you now blow down the recorder with all the holes covered, you can play "do." For the next six notes of the scale, come up the hose, removing one finger at a time. To get the top note of the scale, uncover the thumb hole.

Cut thumb hole directly below top hole

Mouthpiece

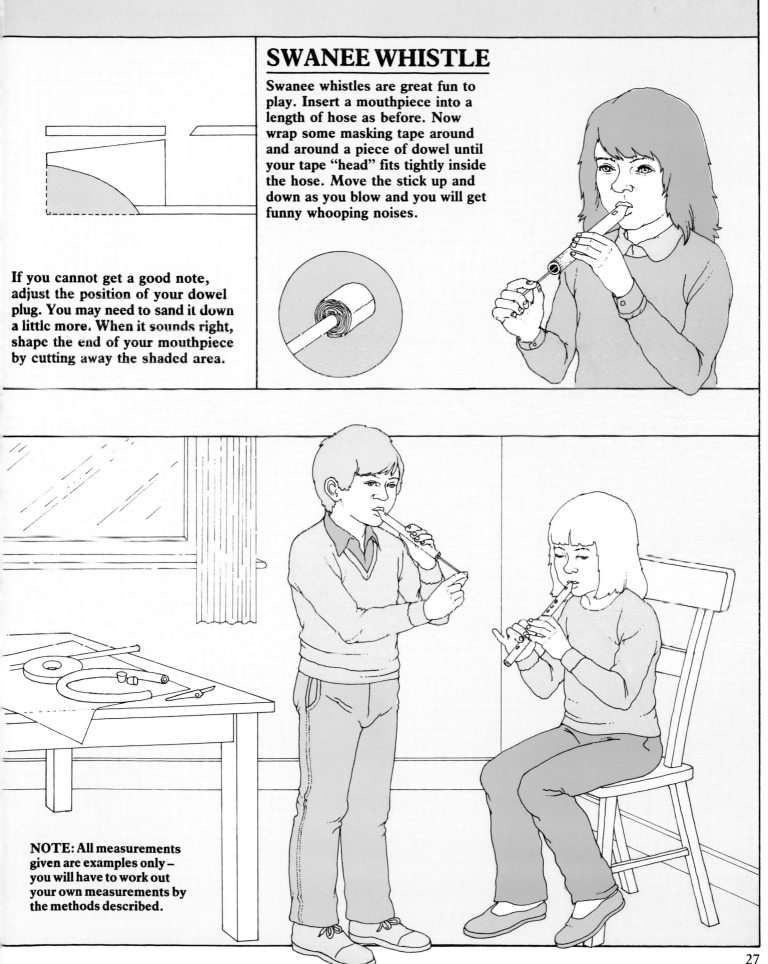

SWANEE WHISTLE

Swanee whistles are great fun to play. Insert a mouthpiece into a length of hose as before. Now wrap some masking tape around and around a piece of dowel until your tape "head" fits tightly inside the hose. Move the stick up and down as you blow and you will get funny whooping noises.

If you cannot get a good note, adjust the position of your dowel plug. You may need to sand it down a little more. When it sounds right, shape the end of your mouthpiece by cutting away the shaded area.

NOTE: All measurements given are examples only – you will have to work out your own measurements by the methods described.

EIGHT-STRING ZITHER

In its simplest form a zither consists of a flat sound box with strings stretched over it. It is laid flat on a table or across the musician's lap when played. A concert version may have up to 45 strings, four or five of which run across a fretted finger-board. These few strings provide the melody and are plucked between the thumb and forefinger of the right hand or with a plectrum. The other strings are used for accompaniment only.

You will need: A strip of wood measuring about 36 × 1¼ × 1¼ inches (90 × 3 × 3 cm); a sheet of strong cardboard; a dowel; wire; eyelet screws; nails; Stanley knife; masking tape; glue; sandpaper; bits of foam rubber.

ZITHER INSTRUCTIONS

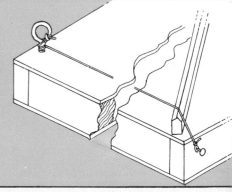

1: A frame for the sound box can be made from four strips of wood – two 9½ inches (24 cm) long and two 7 inches (17 cm) long. Carefully smooth the sawn edges with sandpaper.

2: Glue the strips of wood onto the cardboard to make a rectangular base for your box. When dry, trim away any excess cardboard with a Stanley knife.

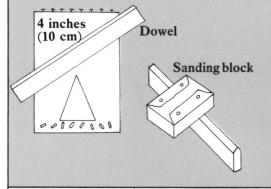

6: Mark a point 4 inches (10 cm) down the side of the frame. Measure the distance from that point to the opposite corner and cut a length of dowel to fit. Sand the dowel into a point.

7: Glue the dowel into position, pointed side up. This forms the "bridge" or support for the strings. Now is the best time to do any varnishing or decorating.

8: Cut lengths of fishing line 4 inches (10 cm) longer than the length of the box. Knot one end around the nail and the other around the screw-eye opposite.

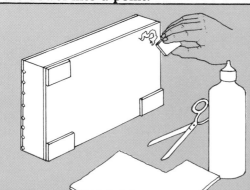

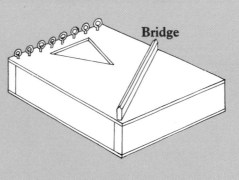

9: When all eight strings are attached, it is a good idea to glue small pieces of foam rubber to each corner of the base. This will improve the sound quality.

Tuning the strings. If you have difficulty tuning the strings by ear to an eight-note scale, try using a piano to help you. Tighten the screws of each string in turn until they sound like the eight shaded piano notes. This method cannot guarantee success, but it might be worth a try!

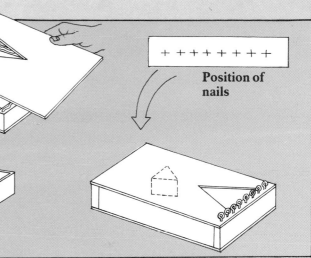

Position of nails

3: Cut out another piece of cardboard to fit over the top of your box (but do not glue!). Mark the position of a triangular sound hole and cut out carefully.

4: Cut a strip of cardboard 3¾ inches (9 cm) long and as deep as the inside of the frame. Bend into three equal parts and tape the ends. Glue onto the middle of the base and add the top.

5: At the sound-hole end, insert eight eyelet screws in the top of the frame. Along the side (NOT the top) of the other end, hammer in a short nail opposite every eyelet screw.

Plucking the strings with the tips of the fingers produces only soft sounds. The wires may also cut into your skin. For these reasons, musicians have developed the plectrum – a small piece of wood or metal held between the thumb and forefinger. You can make a plastic one out of a yogurt container or ice cream carton. Now when you pluck the strings, the sound will be louder and have more "ring" to it.

Plectrum

SIMPLE TUNES AND RHYTHMS

RHYTHM AND BEAT

Rhythm is the way in which musical notes are grouped together in time. When you dance or clap in time to a record, you are picking out the strong beats of the rhythm. As you clap, count out the beats. Every time you hear a very strong beat count 1. The number of beats you can count before you hear the next strong beat is called the number of beats in a bar.

The examples below show four common rhythms. At the left of each example are two numbers (the time signature). The top number indicates how many beats there are in a bar, and the bottom number tells you what kind of note is the equivalent of each beat. For example, 4 on the bottom means quarter notes (see p. 32).

Now practice the rhythms shown. Make sure you give a good, heavy thump for the first beat of every bar. $\frac{4}{4}$ time is a typical marching rhythm, while $\frac{3}{4}$ is the time signature of a waltz. And you might recognize the gentle, rocking rhythm of a lullaby in $\frac{6}{8}$ time.

NOTE VALUES AND RESTS

Different musical notes have different time values. Look at the box below. Starting from the bottom, a whole note is worth twice as many beats as a half note, a half note twice as many as a quarter note, and so on up to the top. Note that eighth notes and shorter-length notes can be written separately or as groups. A dot after a note lengthens that note by half its value. For example, a dotted half note is worth three quarter notes, not two.

It is also important to write down musical silences of definite length. The marks that represent a silence are called rests. Every musical note has an equivalent rest.

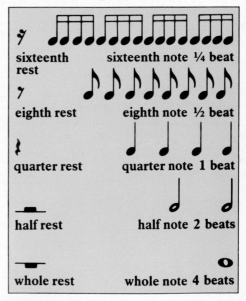

sixteenth rest	sixteenth note ¼ beat
eighth rest	eighth note ½ beat
quarter rest	quarter note 1 beat
half rest	half note 2 beats
whole rest	whole note 4 beats

NOTATION

Musical notes are given the name of the first seven letters of the alphabet. They are placed on a staff (the name given to the five lines) as shown.

C D E F G A B C D E F G A

SIMPLE TUNES

You can play simple songs on any of the tuned instruments you have made. If you cannot read music, don't worry. Look at the diagrams at the beginning of each tune to find out where the notes are on your instrument. The fingering charts at the beginning of *When the Saints* will show you how to play the notes on your recorder.

FRÈRE JACQUES

Always look at the time signature before you start playing. Ask your friends to join in. They could sing or play other instruments.

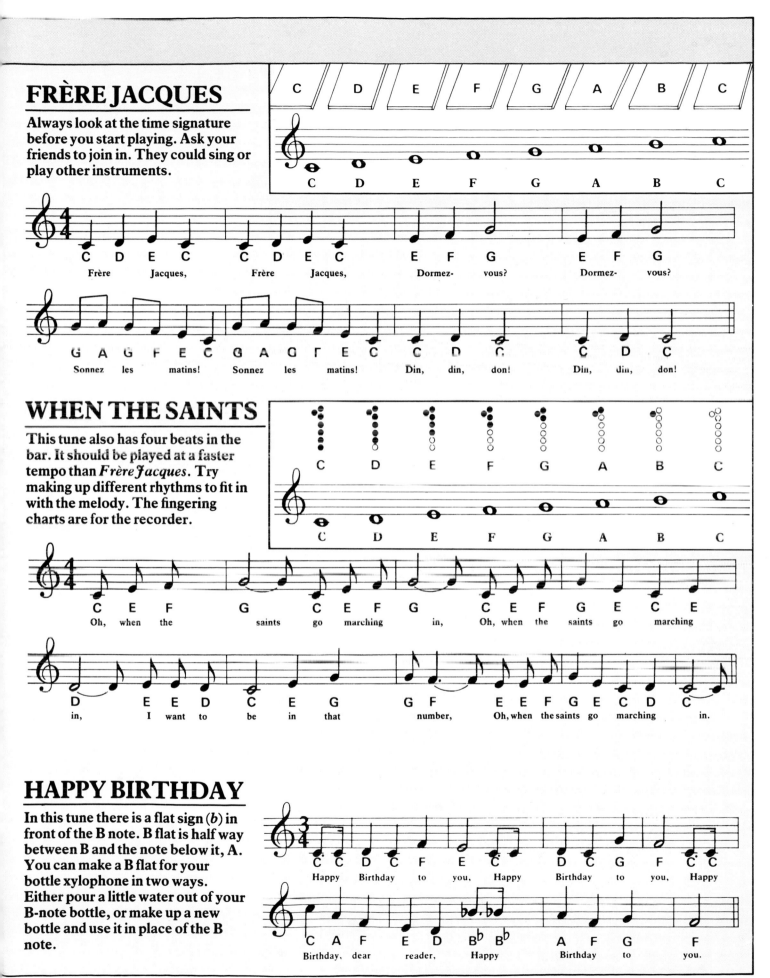

C D E F G A B C

C D E C C D E C E F G E F G
Frère   Jacques,   Frère   Jacques,   Dormez- vous?   Dormez- vous?

G A G F E C G A G F E C C D C C D C
Sonnez les matins! Sonnez les matins! Din, din, don! Din, din, don!

WHEN THE SAINTS

This tune also has four beats in the bar. It should be played at a faster tempo than *Frère Jacques*. Try making up different rhythms to fit in with the melody. The fingering charts are for the recorder.

C D E F G A B C

C E F G C E F G C E F G E C E
Oh, when the saints go marching in, Oh, when the saints go marching

D E E D C E G G F E E F G E C D C
in, I want to be in that number, Oh, when the saints go marching in.

HAPPY BIRTHDAY

In this tune there is a flat sign (b) in front of the B note. B flat is half way between B and the note below it, A. You can make a B flat for your bottle xylophone in two ways. Either pour a little water out of your B-note bottle, or make up a new bottle and use it in place of the B note.

C C D C F E C D C G F C C
Happy Birthday to you, Happy Birthday to you, Happy

C A F E D B♭ B♭ A F G F
Birthday, dear reader, Happy Birthday to you.

MUSICAL DIRECTORY

MUSICAL TERMS

Bar Beats (*see below*) usually group themselves into regular patterns, which are divided by *bar lines* into bars or measures. A *double bar* indicates the end of a piece of music.

Beat A regular musical pulse.

Clef A sign placed at the beginning of each staff (*see below*) which fixes the pitch (*see below*). The treble clef contains higher pitched notes than the bass clef.

Duet A piece of music performed by two players.

Eighth Note A note that has a time value of half of a quarter note.

Embouchure The way in which the lips are shaped around the mouthpiece in a wind instrument.

Fermata A sign placed over a note to increase its time value.

Flat A sign placed in front of a note to lower it by a half step (for example, B♭ sounds halfway between the notes B and A).

Half Note A note that has a time value of two quarter notes.

Harmony The sound of two or more notes played together.

Melody The tune that can most easily be picked out in a piece of music.

Pitch How high or low a note sounds.

Plectrum A small piece of wood or metal used to pluck strings.

Quarter Note A note that has a time value of one beat in $\frac{4}{4}$, $\frac{3}{4}$, and $\frac{2}{4}$ time, equal to one fourth of a whole note.

Reed A thin, flexible piece of cane or reed found in some wind instruments. Sound is produced as it vibrates.

Rest A sign that represents a musical silence of definite length. Every note has an equivalent rest.

Rhythm The way in which notes are connected in time.

Scale A series of notes written in order of pitch (*see above*).

Sharp A sign placed in front of a note to raise its pitch by a half step (for example, F♯ sounds halfway between the notes F and G).

Sixteenth Note A note that has a time value of a quarter of a quarter note.

Staff A five-line grid on which musical notes are written to indicate pitch (*see above*).

Tempo The speed of the music.

Time Signature Two numbers, one on top of the other, placed at the beginning of a piece of music. The top number shows how many beats there are in the bar; the bottom number tells you the type of note that equals one beat.

Whole Note A note that has a time value of four quarter notes.

ORCHESTRAL INSTRUMENTS

The modern symphony orchestra may have more than 30 different instruments and over 100 musicians. Toward the front of the orchestra are the strings, which make up about half of the instruments. Near the middle is the woodwind section, while the brass and percussion are at the back. Any solo performers, such as pianists or singers, are placed nearest to the conductor at the front.

Every section of the orchestra is represented by instruments in this book, except for the brass. But once you understand the principles of how sound is made in each type of instrument, you may be able to work out homemade versions of your own. A kind of horn, for example, could be made from a plastic funnel fixed into the end of a piece of garden hose. See how many other kinds of instruments you can invent.

Strings
Violins
  – First violins
  – Second violins
Violas
Cellos
Double basses

Woodwind
Piccolos
Flutes
Clarinets
Bass clarinets
Oboes
English horns
Bassoons

Brass
Horns
Trumpets
Trombones
Tubas

Percussion
Indefinite pitch instruments
  – Snare drums
  Tenor drums
  Bass drums
  Cymbals
  Triangles
  Gongs
  Tambourines

Tuned instruments
  – Timpani (or kettledrums)
  Xylophones
  Glockenspiels
  Chimes
  Vibraphones
  Marimbas
  Celeste

Sound effects
  – Wood blocks
  Rattles
  Sleigh bells
  Castanets, etc.

Occasional instruments
Piano
Harp
Guitar